SERVICE AS A WAY OF LIFE™

Ignite the fire of love to truly be of service.

By utilizing the gems of exquisite self-care on a daily basis
and honoring your truth, your mission of service is born.

SERVICE AS A WAY OF LIFE COPYRIGHT

Please note:

The written or spoken information, ideas, procedures and suggestions contained and presented in 'SERVICE AS A WAY OF LIFE' workshops and books are meant for educational purposes only and are not for diagnosis. It should not be used as a substitute for your physician's advice. 'SERVICE AS A WAY OF LIFE' is not therapy and is not intended to replace the recommendations of a licensed health practitioner. It is the responsibility of the reader to consult with their own medical Doctor, Counselor, Therapist or other competent professional regarding any condition before adopting any of the suggestions in this book.

SERVICE AS A WAY OF LIFE™

Dedicated to the heartfelt desire to be of service in the world, fueled by wisdom, generosity and a deep seated love for the self.

MISSION STATEMENT

To guide and facilitate women
in becoming their most beautiful and radiant selves.

To acknowledge and embrace the well of love
and power which lies within all women and to ignite the
awakening and embodying of this life force.

To empower each woman, through exquisite self-care and love,
to live her fullest life possible, and to walk her path of wisdom
and truth, as she shares this light and knowledge
with all beings.

IN DEEP GRATITUDE
Thank you

The creation, birth and life of 'A Woman's Truth' would not have been possible without the love, support and devotion from the following angels in my life:

My beautiful daughter Megan who naturally embodies the teachings of living in her truth and integrity, thank you for the creative gift of the beautiful artwork. Helena Nelson-Reed for her generosity of spirit in allowing her extraordinary artwork, which embodies the teachings so magnificently, to grace the covers. Dennise Marie Keller for her unwavering support and dedication to the teachings and for proofing, editing, aligning and translating my vision into the technical world of manifestation. Dan Fowler for his creative genius and dedication. Lucy Alexander and Suzanne Ryan, my dearest friends for their amazing editing and wholehearted encouragement. Monica Marsh for her commitment, support and belief in the workshops. Maggie Crawford, my mum, for her proofing and for being a living example of the teachings. Cait Myer and Katie Steen for their patience and ability to decipher my handwriting and for formatting the books. Bethany Kelly for her support. Deborah Waring for holding the space for the conception of 'A Woman's Truth' to be born and for her insight in the first year of teaching and Emmanuel for believing in my vision.

My mentors and teachers Rod Stryker, Adyashanti and Alison Armstrong, Max Simon and Jeffrey Van Dyk for their continuous and guiding light in my life, their never-ending belief in my potential and for always teaching me the way to evolve into my highest and most potent self. And to all of you beautiful and courageous women who are committing to living your truth and transforming into your most radiant selves,

thank you.

A PRELUDE

An overture to service as a way of life.

Being of service to others is the primary way we as women have traditionally expressed our love and established our value in society. However, many women have never had the luxury, or the time, to stop and ask whether the way in which we serve others is truly in alignment with our highest calling or destiny.

Through her inspiring and thought-provoking work, Miranda Barrett invites you to take an inward journey into the depths of your soul in order to find a way to be of service *while* fulfilling your destiny. The exercises she presents will gently walk you through the process of discovering the unique ways you were destined to serve.

Divine service leads to joy and fulfillment in life, but it requires self-care as its principle foundation. In fact, service and self-care are inextricably linked in a cyclical process that must be honored in order to create true balance in life. Miranda encourages you to demonstrate self-care (in the form of honoring your truth), which leads to an increased level of service (in the form of living your highest destiny). When you live your highest destiny, your service (in the form of expended energy) increases your need for self-care (in the form of rest, retreat, and rejuvenation).

As a holistic energy therapist for intuitive and psychic children, I completely live the joy of honoring my destiny through divine service. Yet, I understand first-hand that the urge to over-give and over-serve is ever present. The risk of burnout, especially among those who love what they do for a living, is exceptionally high. I cannot express how grateful I am to Miranda for her guidance and support in helping me live a balanced life by attending to my need for self-care.

Your willingness to follow intuitive guidance from the Divine is the key to finding the balance between service and self-care. I can think of no better teacher than Miranda Barrett to help you awaken your destiny and nurture your ability to turn within and discover the path that will lead you to a life you can love.

~ Niki Elliot, Ph.D
Founder, Innerlight Sanctuary
www.innerlightsanctuary.com

When Miranda Barrett's book came into hands, it was beyond timely. My mother and I had just placed my father into a memory care facility after a 3-year, very rapid decline into Dementia/Alzheimer's.

Making the decision to take my father from the home he had lived in for 23 years with my mother, and after 50 years of marriage, was perhaps one of the toughest challenges we had ever faced as a family. Because my two older brothers were too far away to help except through support over the phone, it was up to my mother and me (and my dear husband) to try to manage. Those traumatic two months as care facility after care facility failed to help my father adjust were exhausting.

As of this writing, we are still in the midst of a very tough time, and as of yet, we have no idea where or what can possibly help the situation. What I am learning is that sometimes, a pause in the action does not come. Sometimes in life, we will be faced with situations that are relentless in their dire nature, and the stress and shock, grief and challenge can remain at high levels for stretches of time formerly unimaginable. However, we can survive; we can even *thrive,* during times like these, but we can only do so by having our life skills at the ready, and ideally, having them in place well before acute challenge and sudden change.

Miranda's book arriving so perfectly in my reality felt like a moment in a film, where a white feather wafts down from some heaven, sing-songing through the air to gently land in one's upturned hands, just at that moment when giving up seems the only choice, and All Seems Lost.

We may each be given a chapter in life when *self-care* eclipses our idea of "Selfless" Service. Indeed, it becomes of the utmost importance; so important that it can be the very difference between Life and Death. Our own death or a loved one connected to us, in a situation that has left them feeling rudderless, abandoned by all that is good, and believing themselves wholly incapable of rising to face another day.

Miranda's 'Service As A Way Of Life,' could also be called, "Self-Care for the Selfless". Self-Care is a tremendous necessity in the times we are living in, and especially for those who see the needs of others and notice the suffering of others, and feel the calling to try to help; almost always to the detriment of their own needs; their own state of health and wellness and balance.

Nevertheless, as the saying goes, first we must help ourselves: if *we* are the one drowning, we cannot possibly hope to take anyone to shore, as desperately as our heart may want to try. *We will surely both go down.*

No matter our spiritual beliefs about why things happen, or what part we are supposed to play in the healing or the lessening of suffering of others, I notice that the body will let us know when it is out-of-balance, and needs our attention. The Heart has no limits. It does not know of the concept "No." or "Done."

It keeps renewing itself, and expanding its limitless limits to include even the indescribable moments of challenge, loss and love. This is why Self-Care must truly come first so the Body can survive our Heart's Hero's Journey, as we continue, fueled by the spirit of Love: which is what fuels a life of Service.

Set aside these moments, one cup of tea at a time, to absorb this incredibly rich, gentle and extremely effective guidebook. Your Mind, Body, and Spirit will be aligned so deeply that no matter the Lows or the Highs, there will always be a center, a Middle Way, a core of stillness and stability guiding you through your journey of Heart in living 'Service As A Way Of Life.'

In Love and Deepest Gratitude for Miranda, and for the Universal Intelligence that moves through each of us, whispering, *"I Love You. You are Worthy of All that is Good. You are Supported by Life. Become Still, Go Within, and Simply Know*

~ **em claire**
Poet and Author of
'Silent Sacred Holy Deepening Heart and Home Remembers Me. '

SERVICE AS A WAY OF LIFE™

Gems of Consciousness

A DAILY PRACTICE
commit to yourself

*F*ollow these simple steps daily as a way to instill and strengthen your heartfelt resolve to love yourself. This will help to keep you aligned, transforming and on track, giving you a stable foundation for the rest of your life. As a gift to yourself, please mark the teachings as you read them through and congratulate yourself with each one. See each day as a commitment to take exquisite care of yourself.

A LIFE WORTH LIVING

"Never give from your well.
Always give from your overflow."
~ Rumi

All too often as women, your own needs are denied for the benefit of others as you orchestrate your life through demands and expectations you feel responsible for. Unfortunately, this can leave you without the juice and energy needed to be present fully and to enjoy life. During these readings, you will continually discover more about who you truly are and learn the tools needed to live your most authentic and fulfilling life possible. From this place, you will experience being 'full to overflowing' and all the joy and energy this brings.

As you delve into these teachings, you will explore, laugh, study, share, and freely express who you are. In this sacred space, you will ultimately learn your truth as a woman in order to shine, to embody your own beauty, believe in your own worth, and take exquisite care of yourself. For only in this way can you truly be of service.

During these guidebooks, many of the basic needs of women will be explored such as sleep, nutrition, creativity, movement and time to replenish. A topic has been chosen for each book and a cohesive and practical foundation is laid out to inspire and guide you. This will bring about a new strength and resolve which will allow your needs to become a priority, without letting your outer world dictate otherwise. By the end of our time together, the concept of being confident, loving, serene and passionate will no longer be a distant fantasy. Instead, these and many other extraordinary qualities that you naturally embody as a woman will flow with ease, grace and love.

With life's demands so high, it has become imperative that your needs are first acknowledged, honored and then taken care of. From this vantage point, your relationship with yourself then has the potential to be transformed into one of self-love. The beauty is this in turn creates a life that not only fulfills you and your life's purpose, but also allows everyone touched by your presence to receive this gift.

I look forward to spending this precious time with you.

Welcome to A Woman's Truth.

Sincerely and with love,

Miranda

ALL WOMEN

I am woman
Hear my cries.

I am woman
Drink from my tears.

I am woman
Bleed from my womb.

I am Woman.
Know my heart, my song, my dance.

I am woman
Know my strength, my soul, my vulnerability.

I am woman
My heart beats and my feet stomp to the rhythm of the earth mother.

I am Woman.
In all my glory, my beauty, my essence.

I am woman
Hear my voice, my scream, my roar.

I am woman
Feel my passion, my sensuality, my life-force.

I am Woman.

I am all women
The living embodiment of fire,
of creation, of life itself.

I am all women
Loved, birthed, honored.

I am all women

The Queen, the victim, the whore.

I am all women
The high priestess, the nun, the child.

I am all women
The mother, the daughter, the crone.

I am all women
In my heart, my soul, my being.

And I pray to us all
To the Divine Mother
Who holds us in her heart and hands?

I pray that we no longer abort and destroy
The power and creation
That is all women.

I pray we as women heal and hold our heads high,
Our hearts open and power in our bellies.

I pray that we use love as our greatest sword,
Self-respect as our shield,
Self-love as our armor
And the grace of compassion and forgiveness is what leads us forward.

I pray that from the eagle's eye we remember all that is possible.
That we as women will rise from the ashes, transformed to be reborn as the phoenix.

I pray that the hopes and dreams of all women
To embody fully whom they are and live their hearts' desire becomes a reality.

I am woman
Do not silence me
Hear my truth.

I am woman
See through my eyes
Feel my love.

I am woman
The feminine, the creator
Full of grace.

I am woman

I am Goddess.

I am.

BEING OF SERVICE

"I slept and dreamt that life was joy.
I awoke and saw that life was service.
I acted and behold, service was joy."

~ Tagore

When you align with your true calling the expression is one of effortless joy. Your existence will become filled with purpose, happiness and grace as you live your life embodied with the talent you were gifted at birth. In contrast, attempting to live someone else's design will often translate into fitting a square peg into a round hole.

As you reveal your own natural capacity and exceptional abilities, your journey will be parallel to the sublime energy of the universe. This in turn will support your destiny and ultimately fill you to overflowing. The simple quality of living your authentic existence will then pour into the lives of others as they receive its gifts and offerings. By living in your essence, you will naturally be of service to others. Being of service is a win-win situation because everyone benefits and receives grace.

"My work is hard to explain. Even after all this time, when someone asks me what I do, I still find it difficult to put it into words. How do you describe being able to see into someone's inner and secret world to fathom what is limiting their light and awareness? Yet this is what I do. Did I learn this from a teacher? No. Is it a gift I have always had? Yes. Can I teach it to you? Not really. Yet it is as easy to me as breathing and as effortless as brushing my teeth. I am sure there are plenty of other jobs I could be good at, but I know this is the one that truly allows me to be of service." ~ Miranda

For some, their calling is obvious. For others it is a life-long search. Yet as you seek to discern and distill what it is that you came here to be, your life will evolve and open up into many adventures and possible miracles and synchronicities. As human beings, there is a strange propensity to be very destination oriented. What is fascinating is for each one the final destination is death. Why then are we in such a hurry to meet this end? Why not slow down the voyage to stave off the final encore?

"Death isn't sad.
The sad thing is: most people don't live at all."
~ Socrates

The philosophy of living a full life is beautifully depicted through the wisdom of being awake to the present moment. This simple teaching will release the past, and stop worrying about the future, allowing you to be conscious enough to live in this precious instant in time.

Remember, you are the author of your own destiny.

If you find yourself desperately unhappy in areas of your life or feel trapped and confined, the chances are that some part of you is not aligned with your mission. Another possibility is you are aligned with your gift, yet are feeling burnt out or unappreciated.

In this second scenario, it is more about perspective rather than the actual rudimentary challenges of your life. Over time, there can be a tendency to no longer appreciate the many bountiful qualities that once seemed so magical and exciting to you. Even if you are doing what you absolutely love, if burdened with it seven days a week, twelve hours a day, you will burn out the love.

There is a theory that it is vital to reinvent yourself every seven years. This seems to play out in the realm of marriages, with the 'seven year itch' and in the domain of work. This does not necessarily mean that you need to change completely what you are doing, although for some people this may be the case. It is more about bringing back the essence of creativity, passion, reinvention and transformation that birthed the situation in the first place. A sense of gratitude and appreciation is certainly the potent first step to rebuilding your foundation.

Therefore the primary question to ask is:

How do you marry your mission and purpose with being of service?

Before this can be answered, it is vital to inquire and reveal what your true calling really is. Even if you are someone who feels deeply connected to your authentic design, it is still a potent and revealing disclosure to ask the question anyway.

If money is a motivating factor, which it often needs to be, it will eclipse many of your dreams, possibilities or options. By simply playing with the idea of gifting yourself financial freedom, allows your visionary and creative self to emerge, spread her wings and guide you to the highest mountain or the stillest lake. There, your true heart's desire can be revealed. One of the simplest ways to connect to your calling is to ask yourself:

what would I joyfully do for free on a regular basis?

LIVE THE LIFE YOU LOVE

"Be the change you want to see in the world."
~ Gandhi

Remember, you are the mistress of your life. You get to choose how your existence unfolds. Granted the journey sometimes takes a twist and an unseen turn. Yet if you are standing strong in your own center, clear about your path ahead, then the bumps in the road can be handled and smoothly navigated. In addition, if you are no longer jeopardizing yourself through self-sacrifice and self-loathing, then other people's dramas and tragedies will not be able to pull you down.

Imagine you are floating in a boat. You love your boat and take beautiful care of her. You pay attention to the leaks and fix them. You prevent new holes by maintaining her well. You know the direction you are traveling. You have paused the momentum long enough to reveal this course as your life's calling. You have inquired and sought answers and insights. At times, you even let go of the oars and let the tides and currents float your boat.

Then all of a sudden, you come across a whole constellation of drama and conflict. Many people from your life or from your past are flailing around in the waters ahead of you. Some in boats that they have not loved, cherished or maintained, others are swimming alone in tides not of their making.

What are you to do?

Throw some life rafts? Pray? Let them all into your boat where their fights and imbalances will capsize your world? Pick and choose whom you let in, the young, the old, the favorite? Do you choose to sink your world to save others? Do you keep enabling? Or do you stay in your power and truth by offering tools to help them become accountable and responsible for themselves? Perhaps you just keep paddling!

"The savior becomes the victim of the victim."

This statement has an insidious backlash. The savior archetype of your being is always ready to rescue another. Yet in reality when the drive to save is not for everyone's highest good, the power and strength of the hero is undermined by the need and desperation of the victim. In this conflict, the victim then becomes all-powerful in her victimhood. As the savior tries to fight and battle in a realm not of her making, she does not have the tools nor the insights to navigate the world of the sufferer. Ultimately, the Good Samaritan loses and eventually becomes a victim herself. In this scenario, nobody receives a blessing or a way out.

Then there is the archetype of the martyr. There may be an area of your life where you are playing the injured party and you are possibly capsizing someone else's healthy boat. Everyone is a spectrum of the whole. This means the qualities of the hero, savior, victim, bully, blamer or one who capsizes, are all lying either awake or dormant in your being. The point is which aspect of yourself do you want to re-enact and play out?

"There have been times where I was the drowning, hysterical body in the river of life. Yet, in my experience, if I find a way to haul myself out of the quagmire of my own drama, I am much less likely to fall back into the old pattern again. By calling on my own strength, power and resources, I become my own savior and hero. Even more importantly, I become open to learn a new life lesson, and to change. Ultimately, a new resolve is born, and I reclaim my own boat." ~ Miranda

You can change the tides of your existence. By having compassionate self-discipline you can bring in a new level of consciousness to any situation. Do you choose to be angry while standing in line because you are in a hurry or do you spend the few minutes doing some kegals and focusing on your breath or posture?

"Whenever I am waiting in a long line at the market, I read my horoscope in all the magazines at the checkout. By the second or third one, I get the rough gist of my possible month or week ahead. Time well spent!" ~ Miranda

When choosing to live the life you love, it is imperative to clear out redundant behaviors, areas and actions. This includes people who cause you misery. What in your life do you dread having to do or who do you loathe having to see?

The question to ask yourself here is:

why are you still torturing yourself?

Is there a way to delegate the actions or to eliminate the person lovingly? Yes, there are always times in life where it seems there is no choice. Yet, instead of being in the company of wolves, you can always prepare yourself and limit the exposure.

"There are a few chores I cannot stand and unfortunately cleaning house is one of them! I cannot tell you the pleasure and joy it gives me to have my house cleaned and not by me. There have been times where money is tight, yet I still decide that keeping my wonderful cleaning lady is definitely worth more than eating out or a new pair of boots." ~ Miranda

When you understand that you are the captain of your ship, you may realize that you choose the speed, direction and ocean you travel in. As a grown woman, there is literally no one else to blame if you are heading in the wrong direction.

LOVE THE LIFE YOU LIVE

Gratitude is the foundation to a life fulfilled.

$\mathcal{H}$ave you ever tried to follow a recipe, without the basic ingredients? Especially in the world of baking, this can be a disaster. Try making a delicious, moist, chocolate cake without any chocolate, eggs, butter or flour… no cake!

A life without gratitude is like apple pie without the apples. If this vital ingredient is missing in the recipe called life, there is no foundation for manifesting your dreams. The simple act of being deeply thankful for what you already have allows any new vision or idea to be infused with the most fertile of life's gifts, gratitude.

"In my own life, I notice that when I bathe in a deep sense of gratitude, I have a greater vision and an inner strength which allows me to believe that anything is possible. When I see my life as already full, I am coming from a place of abundance and contentment. This calms the survival aspect of my brain, which strongly believes there is not enough to go around. In this place of lack, it is as though my viewfinder shrinks and I am no longer able to hold the strength and resolve to manifest my dreams. As soon as I bring in gratitude, it is as though I can breathe fully again. The sun figuratively starts to shine and I feel I have everything I need to complete my life. Strangely enough, in the moment of inviting in gratitude, the only thing that actually changes is my attitude. Yet the gifts bestowed upon me while in this space are priceless." ~ Miranda

In comparison, if you feel angry and resentful about your life, any new vision or dream, (especially a really juicy one), will seem a far-off fantasy and unreachable. The response to these limiting emotions may make it impossible to bridge these two worlds. Again, gratitude is the cure-all and with only one side effect, which is more dreams becoming reality.

"When I was eighteen, I decided to get a tattoo. I chose a symbol from a Chinese oracle called the 'I Ching'. After maybe a little too much whiskey for liquid courage, I embarked on my adventure. The next morning I awoke to find that the work of art was not 'The Wanderer' I had chosen. I spent the next half hour going through the 'I Ching' text to find out what I had tattooed on my arm. In disbelief, I discovered it was the symbol for 'Joyous Lake'.

It is important at this point to fill you in. There was nothing joyous or lake-like about my life at this point. In fact, I was angry, rebellious and in a dark place. Therefore having been tattooed for life with a beautiful serene image instead of the rather stark wanderer, felt like a cruel joke. Yet today, I am deeply grateful that the universe or some aspect of my Higher Self gave me the gift of a tattoo 'full to overflowing'. The energy of a joyous lake is certainly a better option than forever expressing the dark night of my soul on my arm." ~ Miranda

This was a prime example of the Higher Self leading the way and was surely a triumph of gratitude winning over resentment.

Are you harboring a dream not yet realized?

In fact, if your life is too far removed from this dream, it might feel like a cruel twist of fate to even contemplate your reality could be so grand. Imagine having a fantasy of being a millionaire when in reality you are living in fear and debt. Many a life's testimony from people who have actually manifested their dreams and aspirations often include the practice of gratitude. As they struggle and strive toward their goal, the quality of appreciation for all they have is kept fully alive.

Another interesting piece around the journey of thriving and succeeding in your life's work is the shadow side of failure. It is often through mistakes, lessons and pitfalls that the true way ahead becomes crystal clear. How often have you said to yourself 'I will never do that again'? This simple statement will propel and send you fiercely in the opposite direction. This more than likely will be highly attuned and parallel to your life's authentic path.

"For a period of my life I was intrigued by what made someone successful. Every person I talked to would share with me some deep dark failure from their past which was the catapult for their future successes. This has always given me a safe haven in the storm when I am forging ahead and seem to be tripping along the way. It seems the line between success and failure is thinner than we would like to think."
~ Miranda

Life sometimes has a funny way of manifesting a desire. For you to reach your goal, the necessary steps may not seem clear to you at the time, but remember the universe does have a plan! The qualities of gratitude and self-love coupled with a clear vision or intention will anchor your dream and will become powerful allies in helping to move you forward.

With gratitude as your core foundation,
you have all the ingredients for an extraordinary life.

DIVINE PRESENCE AND PURPOSE

I establish my divine presence here on earth
I accomplish my divine purpose here on earth.

Have you ever been drawn to someone out of deep respect and admiration and wondered about the appeal and attraction? Often this appreciation is not attached to outside appearances, but more connected to how this person feels and inspires you. It is highly probable that it is associated with how they live their life.

Quite likely, this person is dedicating to and is achieving their authentic vision of whom they are in this lifetime. Let go of the Dalai Lama's and Oprah Winfrey's of this world. Yes, they are both extraordinary living embodiments of accomplishing your Divine purpose. Yet what is being brought to light here is whether **you** are actually living and fulfilling the gifts, desires and talents that you were generously born with.

The secret to living your life fully is to have enough self-love, and self-respect to believe abundantly in yourself. This will give you the tools, energy and clarity to accomplish and actually manifest your life's vision. Have you ever tried to fulfill a dream when you are tired, hungry, afraid and PMS-ing? The chances are you would not have the desire, inclination or energy to even ignite a spark of creativity or will, let alone follow it through. It seems the same message is being played repeatedly that to manifest a great life; the physical body desperately needs to be honored, listened to and taken care of.

When you are triggered into survival mode, your life's purpose becomes that of survival. There is no room for any lofty or grand ideas. Therefore, the trick is to move out of survival and into the higher realms of human existence. Interestingly, you may have the slight sense of a nagging jealousy accompanied by the feeling of awe you have for someone in their power. If so, pay attention that you are not alone.

Jealousy is a sure sign that you may not be happy with an aspect of your life. See this emotion as a powerful teacher. Jealousy is the intrinsic belief that someone else has what you want and that you are afraid there is not enough to go around. With this insight, instead of giving yourself a hard time for being 'jealous', use it as a clue to guide you in the direction of an unfulfilled heart's desire. Rather than being envious, bring your attention back to your life and see how you can give yourself what you wanted in the first place.

One of the genius designs of being human is everyone is original and unique. No two people are the same and there is more than enough to go around. This knowledge can take you out of the limiting survival belief that there is only one bone per dog or one man per woman. This gives you the freedom to live out your individual gift and know there are still thousands of other opportunities available.

One of the intrinsic parts of fulfilling your life's path is that you have a clear vision for yourself, which is supported and nourished by the three following qualities:

◆ A sense of self-love, self-worth and approval.

◆ Enough space and stillness to allow the dream to grow.

◆ An underlying gratitude for all that you already have.

This triangle will catapult and ignite such a fire under your vision quest that it can only rise and become a reality. Then you will become one of 'those' people who you secretly admire, but until now, you were not quite sure what their magic was. Now you know.

"At the center of your being you have the answer;
you know who you are and you know what you want."
~ Lao Tzu

GIFTS OF SELF-ACCEPTANCE

One of the essential aspects of living a full, happy life is the belief you actually deserve one and trusting in the support of the universe.

Have you ever noticed how certain people actually seem to believe that their life should be hard? It is as though they believe that keeping themselves in the limited role of victim and survivor will serve them on some level. It is vital for you to recognize any old beliefs that support you only deserving a small and miserable life. These old tapes will limit your ability to open up your energy field to encompass all that is potentially there for you to receive.

It is as though you are dying of thirst out in the desert. Yet you so strongly believe that the beautiful sparkling oasis in front of you is a mirage, that you do not even attempt to find out if it is real, let alone drink from it. This limitation will come from the idea that you do not deserve to live a life that would nourish and support you.

The question to ask here is:

Do I actually believe I deserve a life that I would thoroughly love and enjoy?

If the answer is yes, then the following pages will give you tools to help fulfill your vision. If the answer is no, then the expression 'misery loves company' needs to be looked into. If you find you strongly identify with the idea of being a victim, pay attention. By holding onto a 'poor me' attitude or the lament of 'why me?' or 'life is hard', you allow these convictions to echo through your mind and continue to be your reality. Take heed to see if you are stifling your life with your beliefs. Remember self-love is the medicine that can turn your direction around.

As you come to truly believe in your worth and live in the essence of deserving a good and inspirational life, you will embody this energy and receive gifts back like an echo. It really is that supremely simple:

◈ **Love yourself.**

◈ **Know you are worthy of it all.**

◈ **Pause long enough to receive the love and support that is readily available.**

Ultimately, love and support yourself and your dreams by consciously taking exquisite and beautiful care of yourself. This will embody and strengthen the belief that you do deserve a beautiful, blissful, bountiful and joyous life. Imagine that!

PERMISSION TO SHINE

Happy in Your Own Boots.

*O*ften in life, the default is to look to others for approval. If they seem proud, then you will give yourself permission to feel good about yourself. During graduations, you may well accept the honors and acclaims, yet in daily life do you pause long enough to become your own advocate? When was the last time you gave yourself credit for just being a decent human being for a day, let alone praising yourself for all that you have accomplished?

Along with gratitude, a sense of accomplishment is another vital part of your foundation. As you begin to align with your purpose, it is fundamental that at each junction you stop and appreciate all that you have experienced or endured to get to where you are today.

Human beings are made up of many experiences, some good and some bad. For you to be reading this is a wonderful triumph and declaration of love for yourself. Yes, the voices in your head will have all sorts of opinions that you are not accomplishing enough. Did you actually do a pajama day? What about doing emails at ten-thirty at night? The point is to focus on all that you have changed, owned and embodied as an expression of self-love, throughout this journey of 'A Woman's Truth'. Take this moment to notice how much more conscious you already are.

Sleep is a good example. You now know exactly how much you really need and it may well be more than you were getting. Even if you do not achieve this every single night, you now have a much stronger relationship with this basic survival need. It really is as simple as the saying goes:

"Is the cup half empty or half full?"

◆ A wonderful fulfilling experience is to take a moment at the end of each day to notice and revere yourself for all you have accomplished.

◆ Fully sink into this feeling.

◆ Notice how this simple act gives you life force. It is as though you are literally filling yourself up.

Another good question to pose is:

Does the cup have cracks in it?

If so, how do you fix the holes and get your cup to the point of full to overflowing? Self-incrimination will cause deep breaks in the cup. When you notice you did not accomplish everything on your list or maybe you committed a misdemeanor that day, forgive yourself. Remember the judge will empty your well just as fast as you can fill it.

You may have witnessed how some of the critical voices in your head have a specific person connected to them. If you imagine these opinions as a committee, it is good to spend a moment discerning if this group of people is there as advocates or critics. Often your mother, father, a teacher or even a boss depicts these voices.

In any moment, you can choose to give them a golden handshake and with gratitude in your heart, let them know that it is now time for them to retire. Then you can choose to invite in a brand new team. People, sages, mystics who will have your back, love you anyway and would never dream of judging you harshly. Imagine having these champions as your committee. A completely new world could be born.

With appreciation and forgiveness, a magical event will occur. As you become your own advocate and source of approval and pride, you will no longer need it from others. When you receive a compliment or recognition, you will accept it with joy, yet are no longer dependent on others for your wellbeing, survival or acknowledgement. You are ultimately free to support and love yourself. The rest is just icing on the cake.

You know who you are.
You know you are a good person.
You know what you are miraculously accomplishing on a daily basis.
You choose to endorse yourself always.

what more could you possibly need?

FREE WILL

A reality check.

While these teachings are largely about dreaming your highest dream and aspiring to your ultimate calling, it is also important to remember the question:

what belief keeps you from taking the greatest leap of your life?

A bittersweet truth is you were given free will. This can be seen as either a blessing or a curse. You choose whether you are wallowing in past dreams and nightmares or fearing future demons. Ultimately, you choose what actions and attitudes support or hinder you. The moral is you get to choose.

"I often have to laugh at myself. There are days when I get thoroughly stressed and cranky. This is usually because I have overbooked and taken my ability to multitask to some ludicrous new height. I then have to remind myself that I chose to book that client at five-thirty after a day of phone calls, writing, work, cooking and parenting. Moreover, I wonder why I have nothing left to give; why I am exhausted and overwhelmed. Yet no one else booked my day. I did. I work for myself. I schedule myself. Yes, there is the pressure of earning money and my insatiable appetite to create, but did I have to do it all by nine o'clock on a Monday night? I do not think so! I know one of my qualities is that I believe anything is possible. Partner this up with my misguided belief that I have to do it all myself and I create days from hell!"
~ Miranda

Remember, you are the writer, director, producer and the main character in your play called life. You get to write the script and act it out. Hence if your life is not turning out as you envisioned it, change the script, stir the pot, add some spice of life and bring some laughter, joy, passion and affection into your days. Do not wait for someone else to give you these precious gifts.

By manifesting a wondrous journey for yourself, you will naturally attract rewards and miracles. This in turn will enhance the caliber and quality of this extraordinary existence called you.

NORMALITY

Why would you want to be normal?
Normal is simply conforming to the average
or bowing to the opinions of others.

As you ponder your life's calling, it is vital to think outside of the box. Imagine Gandhi, Nelson Mandela or Jesus trying to be normal. The chances are they would never have been able to accomplish all that they did, if they had restricted themselves by conforming to other people's beliefs and opinions.

Perhaps it is time for great leaders
and the pure of heart to become the new normal.

Be conscious of letting go of all the limiting and suffocating beliefs that keep you small. Release the idea that ordinary and average is the way to be. Most extraordinary inventions, organizations and creations were born from a spark of genius, which was then fuelled by courage, a leap of faith and a deep-seated belief that anything is possible. Not much is conceived through conforming to the norm. Miracles are born through an infusion of passion and out-of-this-world envisioning.

"I have spent my life not being normal. As a child, I never really fitted in and as a teenager. I wore the suit of rebellion quite well. I certainly calmed down when I became a mother, but have always found a comfort and serenity in not following the herd. This quality has given me the courage and freedom to walk my own path, without concerning myself about conformity or what others think." ~ Miranda

This is very much about letting go of **'should-ing'** all over yourself and discerning how you choose to live your life. Even if it goes against the grain of what you have expected yourself or others might think. This is the wonder of being a fully-grown adult. You are no longer at the mercy of someone else's dogma and you are free to be as sensible or as outrageous as you deem fit.

The question to ask is:

Am I still trying to fit in to a world that is not authentic to me?

INSANITY

Einstein's Theory of Insanity:
"Doing the same thing over and over again
and expecting different results."

You know you are fulfilling your life's purpose if there are no energy leaks and all beings involved receive a gift and blessing. In comparison, one of the clearest ways to know you are heading the wrong way in life is if you begin to feel and experience pain, severe discomfort or exhaustion. These are all sure signs to stop, pause, contemplate and change direction.

Do you remember a time when you kept on trying to do the same action repeatedly, hoping and praying for a different outcome, but in reality always ending back at square one? This could have been in a relationship, a job or any other situation. Then one day you made a different choice. You changed the equation. You left the relationship, the job or the house and all of a sudden, there was a massive relief. Even if it was mixed with some grief or fear, you felt the possibility of a new beginning as the repercussions of the old patterns began to dissolve and vanish.

Another wonderful analogy for insanity is the story of walking down a road and falling into a pothole. The next day as you walk down the same road you forget about the hole and fall in again. This time you are mad at yourself as you think, 'First fall, shame on the road keeper, second fall, shame on me!' On the third day you remember the hole and very consciously walk around it. On the fourth day, you choose a different road.

This is liberation.

When you have walked the same old path repeatedly and the result is physical, mental or emotional pain, fatigue or torture, know you are heading in the wrong direction. In comparison, when you are living out your purpose and mission, there is lightness of being, a joy and a feeling of deep accomplishment that collaborates with your endeavors.

To be honest, your purpose does not need to be some grandiose concept of changing the world. It could be as simple as shedding light and love wherever you go or leaving the world a better place. Maybe you picked up some trash on your hike today or smiled at a stranger.

THINK OF A TIME YOU HAD A NEW EXPERIENCE:

◆ How did it make you feel?

◆ Did it excite you?

◆ Did it give you energy or take it away?

◆ Could you have done it for hours and not noticed the time of day or were you tired within minutes of beginning?

If something exhausts you on a regular basis, pay attention, as it is a sure sign of not aligning with your higher destiny.

"It always amazes me that when I am passionate and excited by what I am doing, time seems to stand still. My bodily functions and needs seem to disappear and I am in a zone of energy and vitality that flows throughout me. When I am in this space, I know I am fulfilling my Divine Purpose and Mission as I am also being filled." ~ Miranda

FOLLOWING YOUR HEART

Never broken...only opened.

It sounds so easy, just follow your heart and you will be led to your destiny, your purpose or your calling. If only it were that simple. Unfortunately, the feeling of pursuing your heart's desire can often be disguised by many an outlandish imposter who has your survival at heart, not your divine mission. The wounds and experiences from the past can beautifully mimic a heart's calling. What if your heart has been broken? Most of us have experienced heartache through either death or the end of a relationship.

"I remember the first time I felt like my heart was breaking. Deep inside, my chest literally hurt. After many days of my version of eating pints of ice cream, I reconciled some of my pain by deciding a broken heart had more room and capacity to love than an unbroken one. I knew the next person I choose to love would be the richest man alive; as my heart was already broken wide open." ~ Miranda

Therefore, following your heart may seem like sound advice, yet first it is vital to discern if it is your loving or wounded heart leading the way. A broken heart can easily tempt you down the same dark alleyways and into the deserted buildings that you traveled to in the past, desperately seeking the essence of love.

Every experience leaves an imprint. Unless you pour yourself into pure, courageous and unadulterated healing, you may be unaware that old patterns and behaviors are leading you in a direction that will play out like an old broken record. Fearless inquiry has to be performed with the skill of a surgeon on a shattered piece of your being, before you can even possibly know if the calling is purely from your heart or distortedly from your wound.

Remember, survival is a wily fox. It will convince, manipulate and con you into believing its truth. Yet, imagine if your survival instinct, which is extremely powerful, became stuck in a belief at age four. Then the chances are that this undeveloped part of your psyche would not have enough perspective, life experience or wisdom to be driving the bus and making big life changing decisions.

DISCERNING A TRUE HEART:

◈ The point is to do your own healing work.

◈ Spend time diving into past experiences that still have a grip on you.

◈ Write 'Letters of Truth' and burn them.

◈ Acknowledge and honor your feelings.

◈ Sit in forgiveness of yourself and others.

◈ Set yourself free.

◈ Let go of the past and choose to be present to the moment in front of you.

◈ Give yourself the gift of freedom to choose a new future.

Every instant of your life
presents an opportunity to awaken to the present moment.

A true heart calling actually has very little agenda. It has purity to its essence that is untouched by the grappling hands of fear and drama. It is unrelated to the ego or survival and it will cause no harm. It is as though your true heart's desire floats above the density of the mundane world. It will lift you as you soar on the wings of love, encouraging a deep feeling of gratitude, purpose and an abundance of joy.

Trust your higher heart. Its purity will never lead you astray. Do not let fears keep you from living your truth. Your destiny is but a single moment in time yet can also be decades of service. Only your heart knows. It will guide you to your highest truth. Have faith. You are love incarnate.

A LIFE CALLING

Are you living your life calling or the life you were dealt?

There can often be a strong draw to embody certain ways of being. For some their passion is to become a mother or an artist. For others, being of service, earning money or making a difference in the world is their vocation. Yet, these choices are often dictated by a list of should's or should not's. These limiting attitudes can change and determine the tides moving in your life. Unfortunately, this may be in the opposite direction of your true heart's desire.

Your true longing and yearning can be eclipsed as you conform to what you **have** to be or do. Over time, you forget the dream as the 'chop wood and carry water' of life takes its toll. Immersed in responsibility and demands, the fantasy of becoming a poet is buried deep below a pile of bills, responsibilities and deadlines.

Interestingly, the word responsibility can be translated as having the ability to respond to a situation appropriately. The point is to discern if living an unauthentic life is appropriate or if delving deeply into your own being and reclaiming your truth is right action. I believe that everyone comes into this life with a natural gift or talent. It is vital to your well-being and calling for this bloom of passion and ability to be nurtured and supported. If this statement below feels a little too familiar, stop the unconscious roller coaster ride and wake up.

"The lights are on but nobody is home."

INQUIRE INTO YOURSELF:

◈   What did you dream of being as a little girl?

◈   What did you envision for yourself before you got lost on the treadmill of life?

◈   Have you secretly longed for a different existence?

◈   Is there an aspect of yourself yearning to be birthed?

Do not become the walking dead.

This life is a precious gift to be explored fully and expressed.

Look to yourself.

Return to yourself.

From this still, tangible center of your being, remember who you are.

Become a full expression of yourself with joy in your heart.

Live with lightness in your step and passion in your soul.

This is your birthright.

Your legacy.

Your dance.

Reside in the highest and most wondrous aspect of which you came here to be.

INTUITION

Fear screams, intuition whispers.
Become still enough to listen to the wise, quiet voice within.

Your intuition or inner voice will lead you to your life's calling. It may not shout or stomp its feet or have a hissy fit like your emotions, yet that still, strong sense of knowing is always present. It is all about whether you are actually listening.

Everyone is gifted with this inner knowledge. It is a part of who we are as humans. It comes under many names and guises. Someone with a green thumb is an intuitive gardener. A brilliant chef is an intuitive cook. They know exactly what to do, how to do it and usually with no training. It is as though you already know. Someone who is good with money and investments is often listening to their inner knowledge. Is it luck or intuition that you show up at the right place, at the right time, or on a hunch? Who really cares if it wins you your life's dreams?

"My intuition has served me well in this life. Years ago, a dear friend and I were driving up to Scotland in the bucketing English rain. All of a sudden, I was overcome with a feeling of dread and fear and I told her to pull over. Giving me a look, but knowing to listen to my 'witchy powers', as she calls them, we did stop. After about five minutes, I could breathe again and we got back on the road. Only to come upon a twenty-car pile-up that had just happened. We were safe and to this day, I thank my intuition and the fact that I listened to it." ~ Miranda

BE OPEN TO INTUITIVE ANSWERS:

◈ Are you listening to your inner guide or are you always looking outside of the realm of your own being for answers?

◈ Are you so caught in others judgments, wants and needs, that there is no room to listen to your own?

◈ Are you being ruled by your fears and allowing your doubts to take charge?

◈ Do you trust yourself and the inner well of knowledge that resides within you?

◈ What is it that you already know or have always known?

Intuition begins with quieting the mind enough to enable the stillness to speak and be heard. It is about listening to your body and developing a trust in your own warning signs. When you are aware, awake and alive you are standing in your power. This is when doubt, fear and guilt no longer have a hold on you. Listening to your intuition will ultimately set you free. Intuitive experiences can be the crowning glory of living from your center. Tune into the frequency that 'speaks' to you.

There are many ways to be intuitive. For some, it may be a strong sense of knowing or an instinctive wisdom. For others, they may feel it physically in their body such as goose bumps or a nervous belly. Sometimes you may even hear or see what it is you need to know. This sixth sense, as it is called, is often translated through one of the other five senses such as the ears, the eyes or sense of touch.

The wonder is that the body never lies, therefore if you are feeling a surge of energy or a collapse into lethargy, pay attention.

There are many commonly used phrases, which speak of intuitive experiences.

◊   My ears were burning.
◊   I felt it in my gut.
◊   It welled up in my throat.
◊   It broke my heart.
◊   I just knew.
◊   There was a knot in my chest.
◊   My palms itched.
◊   Everything in my being told me.
◊   The hairs on the back of my neck stood up.
◊   It gave me goose bumps.
◊   I was so drawn to do so.
◊   I could not breathe.
◊   I felt it in my bones.

In some of these expressions, your body is speaking to you. In others, it is simply an unquestionable moment of knowing. Begin to pay attention and follow your instincts and insights, even if they do not make sense at the time. They will not lead you astray. Become aware of how this messaging and guidance works for you.

COMING FROM YOUR CENTER

You can only discern right from wrong
if you are standing in your center.

In translation, never make a big decision the day before your period or food shop when you are hungry. Life is full of choices; left, right, straight ahead, reverse or stop. In every moment, a decision is made, either to keep the old way alive or to invest in a new awareness or adventure. The good news is that many of the basic survival needs of the body are automatic, such as breathing, digesting and detoxifying. Yet there is still a responsibility to honor this temple, which houses your being, so it can function at its optimum and ultimately thrive.

If you are tired, hungry and cold, the chances are that a hot cup of double chai latte with whipped cream will be highly appealing. Yet there is always a consequence to any choice or action taken. The damage control can sometimes outweigh the immediate and self-gratifying moment of caffeine and sugar!

I believe that as humans we have a responsibility to keep our physical form, the body, performing at its finest. Then you will remain at your center point and the choices surrounding you will be vividly clear as to whether they will enhance or dishevel you.

As you may have noticed, there is only one vital aspect of your being which cannot be replaced. Another job can be found, a new relationship formed, money can be lost and earned again, a house rebuilt, a car replaced.

Yet the body is the one priceless commodity,
which cannot be restored once destroyed.

As you answer these questions, allow yourself a glimpse into the benefits and hindrances of your world. Contemplate all areas of your life. Sleep, nutrition, exercise, relationships, sex, work, parenting, money, speaking your truth, being in your power, balancing the feminine, masculine and child, intuition, nurturing your physical, mental, emotional and spiritual needs. The following questions will deepen your awareness of where you are living in your life.

ARE YOU ROOTED IN YOUR OWN SENSE OF SELF?

◈ Who or what in your life wastes your time, money or energy?

◈ How much of your life is spent doing tasks that you resent?

◈ With what aspects of your life are you discontented or frustrated?

◈ Which parts of your life would be better revamped or reorganized?

◈ Which aspects of your life are working for you?

◈ Which of these parts of your life are worth building upon?

◈ Which of these aspects do you prioritize as the most important in your life?

◈ What fulfills you?

◈ What are you passionate about?

◈ What would you do for free?

◈ What excites you?

◈ What or whom do you love and cherish?

◈ What or who in your life gives back to you and replenishes you?

◈ How much of your life is spent doing what you enjoy?

◈ What is vitally important to you?

◈ What makes you laugh?

◆ What makes you jump for joy, dance around, feel bubbly and full to overflowing?

Caffeine, sugar and alcohol do not count. The answers to these questions are the keys to your kingdom. Once you reveal the answers, start to incorporate them into your life on a daily basis.

Now fill your life with what gives you joy and energy. Some things will enable you to earn money; others will be for the happiness they bring. Whichever it is, know that life has a ripple effect. As you live your life in the lake of your own exuberant joyfulness, each and everyone who touches your waters receives this gift. From this place, you are truly being of service.

"Right is right even if no one is doing it;
wrong is wrong even if everyone is doing it."
~ Saint Augustine

THE WOUNDED HEALER

Faith and fear cannot hold the same space, the same breath, the same moment. In reality, they cannot coexist together.

Which do you choose to live your life in, love or fear? Before you embark on discovering which mission or purpose is calling your name, there is something important to remember. You may have been living out a certain way of being for many years, which was not actually a calling. In this case, the impetus is caused by a situation or experience demanding a certain behavior. Over time, this contortion becomes part of who you are. As you conformed yourself to adapt and evolve into what was needed, no space was allowed for other patterns of behavior to be lived. Unfortunately, your true path was eclipsed by the demand.

"My father was diagnosed with multiple sclerosis when I was very young. This imprint haunted me throughout my young life and due to unusual circumstances; I became his caregiver early on. This role absorbed and dictated my life so fully that other choices such as going to college were not even on my radar. During this time, I became a brilliant 'caregiver' and many of my seeds as a healer were born. Yet it was not until years later after his death that I realized I actually had a deep loathing for this role. Yes, you could say some of this was a reaction to my childhood, yet I began to realize taking care of someone was not even something I was naturally good at. It was an effort and built resentment. I have no desire to change bedpans or mop up wounds. In fact, I am squeamish! Hence, I never wanted to be a nurse or doctor.

Where this has led me today is that yes, one of my archetypes is that of a 'Healer', but not of a 'caregiver'. I was forced into this role by circumstance and now I am very clear that I would not like to take it on again. Sometimes it is tempting more out of familiarity than anything else, but I consciously choose to accept other roles that resonate with me such as healer, guide or alchemist. What I have realized is that when I stand strong in my real archetype, everyone benefits and there is no leaking of energy as I garner my own light and being." ~ Miranda

As you inquire into the roles you are playing out in your life, it is important to discern whether you are truly aligned with your integrity and authenticity. There are many difficult situations where much is learned through experience. It is vital not to become stuck in certain patterns or behaviors if they no longer serve you.

The predicament is that a traumatic experience leaves you with a deep imprint, a familiarity and a strange unconscious desire to relive it repeatedly. This can be true even if the experience was heart breaking the first round. There is often a strange self-soothing quality to repeating past suffering. The psyche will hunt for familiar replays as a way to heal old trauma, while reliving the experience and changing the imprint by making new choices. With knowledge of these tendencies, unconscious patterns in your life can be reviewed and transformed.

"Count it all joy when you experience all manner of trials and tribulations. Knowing that your faith, which is more precious than gold, is being tested and refined by fire."
~ The Bible

The questions to ask are:

◈ Are you pushing the same buttons of your past because your psyche still does not realize there may be other options or ways of being?

◈ Are you re-enacting your past as a way to heal yourself and find a new perspective?

Where these choices often play out is in the fertile and juicy area of close intimate relationships. It could be a partner, husband, boss, boyfriend or girlfriend. Deeply embodied patterns of codependency or attachment can often lead you back into old habits. Decide if the person in your life is supportive or causing you harm.

Often these people can be 'teachers' and 'button pushers'. Even though they will fall into the category of causing chaos and upset in your life, often they are present to help teach you to let go of an old entrenched behavior.

"Because of the situation with my father, my tendency for years was to pick relationships where I would be needed, because this felt familiar and strangely secure to me. I would often find myself in the role of nurturer, financial provider and the 'healthy' one. Of course, this was all a matter of perspective! Over time and after much inquiry I finally figured out the root cause of this behavior. If they were unwell, physically, mentally or emotionally and they became dependent upon me, then they would never leave. It was quite brilliant really, in a sick kind of way. This calmed the abandonment wound that was triggered by my mother leaving when I was so young.

As you can see, the choices and decisions made were fueled by fear and the survival instinct. As a child, my only safe ground was in keeping my father alive. We could say all my eggs were in his basket. Unfortunately, his basket was not in good shape. Today I am making a very conscious choice to pick healthier, stronger and more balanced relationships in my life.

At times, my 'caregiver' radar still hoodwinks me, yet I choose to keep it on a high alert. What is extremely annoying is that my attraction is so often for the wounded ones. I just have to remind myself again and again that if I truly desire a full and gratifying life they are not the ones to choose." ~ Miranda

Some of these situations and people who come into your life as teachers or a helpful (or not so helpful) guide, will aid in exposing your deepest, darkest and most self destructive wounds, patterns and beliefs. Even though these may not be areas that you relish delving into and investigating, without an acknowledgement of your shadows and dysfunctions, you could be allowing these unconscious fears to dictate many areas of your life.

*Change can only come through awareness
and remember growth is one of the most fertile seeds to happiness.*

ARCHETYPES

Inherited images from the collective unconscious.

Archetypes are ancient universal patterns of behavior, which are embedded in everyone. An understanding of human archetypes can be a valuable tool for self-awareness. There are many kinds and by noticing which ones you relate to strongly, much can be revealed about whom you are and what your purpose is here on earth.

Living out a certain archetype is like choosing to be a particular color from the spectrum of the rainbow. You own every one, yet which stroke of color you choose to be in at any given moment is what allows you to live a conscious life. Remember just as an artist mixes red and blue to make purple, you too can embody many different archetypes at once to support you on your journey.

There are certain archetypes, such as the 'Mother' that are very clear for some. If it has always been a dream of yours to have children and dedicate much of your life force to this purpose, this archetype is in your pallet. For others the archetype of 'Artist' may be your color. You will notice that if you are not living in a creative flow, you begin to dry up. Yet, before you embark upon which archetype calls your name, it is important to remember that you may have been living out an archetype that was not actually a calling. Instead, a situation or past experience may have demanded that you become an expert in a certain field because you had to, not because it was your passion.

List archetypes you feel you are embodying in this lifetime:

Do not think. Just allow the images and words to pop into your head. If one comes through but you do not understand the connection, write it down anyway. It may well be a glimpse into your future.

CIRCLE THE ARCHETYPES THAT JUMP OUT AT YOU:

Administrator	Fool	Mediator	Seeker
Addict	Gambler	Mentor	Scientist
Advocate	Goddess	Messiah	Sheppard
Alchemist	Good Samaritan	Midas	Seer
Architect	Gossip	Miser	Servant
Athlete	Guide	Mother	Slave
Artist	Healer	Mystic	Sorceress, Magician
Beggar	Hermit	Networker	Story Teller
Bully	Heroine	Nun	Student
Craftswoman	Hostess	Nurturer	Supporter
Care Giver	Interpreter	Pioneer	Teacher
Child	Joker	Poet	Trickster
Communicator	Judge	Priestess	Vampire
Companion	Keeper of the Faith	Prince	Victim
Designer	King	Princess	Virgin
Destroyer	Leader	Queen	Visionary
Detective	Liberator	Rebel	Warrioress
Dictator	Lover	Rescuer	Whore, Prostitute
Entrepreneur	Manipulator	Saboteur	Writer
Father	Martyr	Seductress	Wisdom Keeper

Now take a precious moment to answer the following questions. For example, if a storyteller, poet or scribe showed up for you, ask yourself, "Are you carving out time to write? Do you have an audience for your creativity?"

where in your life are these archetypes revealing themselves?

Are you expressing these attributes?

Remember each archetype also has a shadow side. Take the attributes of a nun. On the light side, she could be seen as a child of God, a good person who has dedicated her life to spirituality. Yet the shadow could play out as her being overly self-righteous, prudish and strict. This is not about judgment, but about being aware of all aspects of the self.

In order to be whole and live your life fully, the shadow side needs to be acknowledged and embraced when appropriate. The important point is to acknowledge your dark side, yet not let it become too powerful and turn into self-destruction. Power can be derived from embracing the strength and energy of the shadow and transforming it into self-confidence and an honest expression of how you feel. As with so much of your internal work, this is about inquiry and self-discovery.

Embark on this journey with a sense of adventure and lightheartedness.

These are just windows and doorways into your True Self. The aspect of Higher Self ultimately does not need a label or description. By revealing your archetypes, you are freeing your mind and opening your heart. This will give you insight and resolve on your journey of discovering and living your truth.

THE BEAR MEDITATION
what is emotionally eating you?

In nature, if you were to come face to face with a bear, one option would be to throw some food in its direction to appease its hungry appetite. Then as you stand there watching, the bear growls and postures making it quite clear that it is still hungry. You keep feeding the bear. This dance goes on for a while until you have no food left. You have given all you have, but the old grizzly is still hungry. Next, you become the meal! Unfortunately, this can become an analogy for life. What are you feeding in your world with your time, money or energy that has an endless appetite?

◈ **Take a moment to close your eyes and ask to be shown what person, situation or action is a bottomless pit in your life.**
Get a clear picture of this area of your life, which is draining your energy.

◈ **Remember, it is sometimes appealing to watch the drama play itself out, just as you would want to observe a bear in the wild.**
But in reality you are putting yourself in danger by engaging in this situation.

◈ **Notice what happens when you do not have anything left to give.**

◈ **How does this person or situation react when they are no longer getting their fix from you?**

◈ **Take some deep breaths and consciously resolve to feed no longer dangerous wild creatures in whatever guise they may come.**

◈ **Remember it does not serve either of you.**
It is the responsibility of each individual to hunt and find their own food in a way that is authentic and in alignment with their true essence. Potato chips and hot dogs are not bear food!

◈ **Instead, choose to invest your time, money or energy into you and make whatever necessary changes and adjustments are needed to no longer put yourself in the position of the prey.**

ROCKS AND SAND

Decide what is truly important and the rest will surely follow.

Imagine you have a cylindrical, glass vase. Your job is to fill it with as much sand and as many rocks as possible. This may sound like the story of your life, but you do have choices. You could pour in the sand and place the rocks on top. You could layer them. Yet in reality, the most effective way is to place the rocks in first. Especially the larger ones and then add the smaller rocks into the spaces in between. When all the rocks are situated, slowly pour in the sand and allow it to fill in between the cracks and crevices of the rocks. By using this method, you will have more space with which to play. The sand becomes the filler and both elements work together.

Well, your life is no different. Use the rocks as an analogy for what is important to you. As you figure out your priorities, you can then give them a prestigious position in full view. With your intention and end result firmly in place, the little details, such as the sand, will literally fall into the spaces with very little effort. Synchronicities, coincidences and helping hands will abound.

"I was having an extremely full and demanding year. There had been many blessings along with a huge amount of hard work. It was time for my daughter's college applications and finances to be added to a plate that was already piled high! In fact, the only way I was able to not to be overwhelmed was to imagine I was on tour until January 15. At this point, many timelines and projects were to have been completed. I became acutely aware of my rocks having turned into boulders and my glass vase having become the size of a trashcan.

Yet I kept my eye on each priority. I wrote many lists, prayed and called for all the help and guidance possible. I also gave myself a talking to about gratefully receiving help in any form it came. The amount of helpful people and support that I found was quite miraculous. I knew there was an end to the tunnel and I made sure to book my dates with my spiritual teacher in the spring." ~ Miranda

FIND THE ROCKS OR BOULDERS IN YOUR LIFE:

◆ List your rocks in priority.

◆ Are there a few that can be laid to rest for now?

◆ Is there one that if you focused on it could then be released?

◆ Are you calling in all the help and benefactors that you need?

◆ Are you taking on the rocks and responsibilities of other people?

◆ Are you able to lay these other people's rocks to rest?

◆ Are there some old rocks and sand that are out of date and no longer need to be in the vessel of your life?

◆ Is there a balance between your goals and just being?

The brain is an extraordinary instrument. Yet if it is given too much to handle, it will have to delegate some of the stress to the body. If you have overfilled the bathtub and the overflow is blocked, all that water then pours into the house and causes untold damage. It is the same with an overflow of stress in the body.

By prioritizing and using the rational brain to timeline what at first may seem like a daunting 'to do' list, you can then evolve into a clear, concise list of priorities. Then the day-to-day journey becomes walking this path called life, with all the rocks, sand, boulders and rainbows along the way.

IF I WON A MILLION DOLLARS...

The dreams of tomorrow begin today.

It has been said that when you come to the end of your life, your biggest regret will probably not be that you wished you had worked more. In fact, wishing you had travelled or spent more quality time with a certain person would probably be much higher on the agenda. What is being examined here is if tomorrow was your last day, would you be content with a life well lived or would you be filled with regrets. The point of this exercise is to release the limitations and fears surrounding money from the equation, therefore elevating you out of the world of survival and into the realms of endless and exciting possibilities.

IMAGINE YOU HAVE A MILLION DOLLARS TODAY:

◈ On what would you spend your money?

◈ How would this change your life?

◈ What else would you change in your life?

YOU HAVE GONE ON A SHOPPING SPREE AND...

◈ Are you still doing the same job or was that the first thing to go?

◈ With what would you replace work?

◈ What did you choose that connected you to your real passions?

◈ Are there changes you can make while waiting for your ship to come in?

Look at what is holding you hostage in your life right now.
It might be money, but it may also be fear.
Sometimes, it is simply a matter of prioritizing your universe.

A VISION BOARD

Seeing is believing and believing is manifesting.

The purpose of a vision board is to give you a creative and visual outlet to begin recognizing and then manifesting what you desire in your life. By using simple tools that you have in your home, you can then have a continual reminder of your dreams.

THE ACTIVITY IS SIMPLE:

◆ Sit down with a stack of magazines, catalogs, photos or pictures, a pair of scissors, some glue and an area to design upon such as a large poster board, wall or ceiling.

◆ Leaf through the pictures and advertisements and notice what attracts your eye, your heart or your attention.

◆ Cut out anything that resonates with you, even if you are not sure why. A picture may depict a quality that you want in your life such as love or adventure. A simple word may invoke a new realm.

◆ Once you have accumulated a generous pile of pictures, begin to arrange them on your surface.

◆ You might play with the images before you glue them down, arranging them in an appealing design or format.

◆ You can always add stickers, gems or ribbons to make it become more alive.

It will be most effective and inspiring if you set your reasoning mind on the back burner and just play with the images. You might find some unusual and enticing ideas jumping out at you that you never realized were a part of who you are or who you want to be.

Many people maintain these boards as an ongoing project, constantly adding new ideas and pieces that are intriguing. Place the project in a prominent area of your home, one where you will see it many times a day. The 'work' will be to simply glance at your vision board and drink in the ideas you have placed before you.

Often, people testify that they assembled one of these boards and worked on it for a period of time and then put it away in the closet. Months or years later, the board crosses their path again and they are amazed at the number of ideas or experiences that had already manifested in their lives. The mind is a powerful tool, so remember, energy follows thought.

what will the story of your life look like?

A MISSION STATEMENT

Defining your life's purpose.

$\mathcal{M}$ost successful businesses have a mission statement. With the knowledge that energy follows thought, it makes sense to set a clear intention in this journey called life. This allows you to move in the direction of your life's focus or purpose. Disney is a brilliant example of this. Their mission statement is clear and to the point.

"To make people happy."

The following is 'A Woman's Truth' Mission Statement. It was birthed through the living expression of forming these teachings. The words reflect the essence and the core value that is held as 'A Woman's Truth.'

"To guide and facilitate Women
in becoming their most beautiful and radiant selves.
To acknowledge and embrace the well of love and power
that lies within all Women and to ignite the awakening and embodying
of this life-force. To empower each Woman, through exquisite self-care and love,
to live her fullest life possible and to walk her path of wisdom and truth,
as she shares this light and knowledge with all beings."

Spending time contemplating your personal mission statement is a fascinating and revealing exploration. A mission statement could pertain to your work, your life, your family or to your relationship with yourself. You will notice as you create one that aligns with who you are, it flows into all aspects of your life.

"when my life is over,
I am curious if I will have lived it or just gotten through it."
~ Elise

CLARIFYING YOUR MISSION STATEMENT:

◈ What limiting beliefs keep you in fear?

◈ Which particular belief holds you the most captive?

◈ What in your life is effortless or would you happily do for free?

◈ What did you dream of being as a child?

◈ What contributes to your happiness?

◈ What gives you a sense of worth?

◈ What do you feel your purpose is?

◈ Is your purpose a specific act?

◈ Is your purpose more about your attitude towards life?

◈ What qualities do you naturally embody that bring out the best in yourself?

◆ Are these qualities aligned with what you are doing in your life right now?

◆ Are you living out these qualities?

◆ What statement would annihilate your limiting, fearful belief, rendering it useless and powerless?

This will be your Mission Statement.
Recite this many times a day as a way
to strengthen your new resolve
and to diminish your old negative beliefs.

Remember, every day you have a choice. The same day can be lived out with joy and gratitude or resentment and despair. Sometimes it is not about what you are doing in your life, but rather how you are doing it. Other times it is about making a change in your life and evolving so you can invite the one calling that you have ignored for years.

In addition, your life's purpose does not necessarily have to be how you earn money. Sometimes your job can be the 'bread and butter' that keeps your reptilian brain out of survival mode. Then the knowledge that there is money in the bank to pay the bills enables you to embody and live out your calling in another area of your life, either as an act of service, such as charity work or in your own time, as a hobby or a passion.

"I have encountered people who have literally seemed heartbroken to me because they have annihilated their connection to their passion and creativity out of an overwhelming belief in responsibility. This is often triggered by the need to provide for themselves or especially, for their family. In many ways, this is admirable and shows an extraordinary strength of character, yet the tragedy is that they are not able to express their deepest desires, thus leaving them without any true vitality and spark for life." ~ Miranda

REVEAL MORE TRUTH

"This is your life. And nobody is going to teach you.
No book, no guru. You have to learn from yourself.
It is an endless thing, it is a fascinating thing
and when you learn about yourself, from yourself,
out of that learning wisdom comes.
Then you can live a most extraordinary,
happy, beautiful life."
~ Krishnamurti

Remember, throughout the time ahead, as you inquire into your life calling and begin to fully live out your vision, keep your judge and critic on the 'down low'. The aspect of yourself that tends to criticize and disapprove of you will not necessarily support your dream of a bountiful, creative and service filled life flowing with grace. The foundation of gratitude, self-love, self-worth and a deep-seated feeling of approval for yourself is what will support the fruition of your mission, becoming your reality and allowing you to be of truly service.

ALLOW THE FOLLOWING TO GIVE CLEAR GLIMPSES INTO THE BLUEPRINT YOU ARE BORN TO BE.

◆ **Please read through your written work.**
  This will keep you aligned with delving deeper into your being. Your purpose and mission can sometimes be buried deep below the surface. Imagine you are mining for gold. Layers of dirt and crud are hiding the shiny aspect of your being. Reading the written work and doing your Truth Work are literally the tools and energy you need to dig for the gold. (Or diamonds if that is what resonates!)

◆ **Enjoy playing with the exercise of receiving a million dollars and see how this would change your world.**

◆ **Envision for yourself what a perfect day, week or month would look like.**
How far removed is this from your practical or real life?

◆ **Spend some time with the archetype list. With which ones do you resonate?**
If a certain archetype keeps revealing itself, pay attention.

◆ **Lastly, decipher what your mission is here on earth.**
This may sound like a tall order, but getting a glimpse of your mission will align
your energies with its manifestation.

During this opportunity to inquire, much can be revealed.
This is an internal gift that you are giving to yourself to live the fullest life possible.

Wishing you the blessings of living the life you love and loving the life you live,

Miranda

ABOUT MIRANDA

A spirited guide and mentor.

Miranda is a passionate and devoted leader. Her loving and wise support will guide you on a transformational journey as her powerful teachings unveil the truth of who you are. Her gift is to offer potent tools, which inspire exquisite and beautiful self-care and empower you to live the fullest and most authentic life possible. As a mentor and guide, Miranda deeply walks her talk and is fearless about her own path of self-discovery, as she weaves the sacred into the mundane.

The simple, yet powerful premise offered by the mystic Rumi is the foundation of Miranda's philosophy and mission:

"Never give from the depths of your well,
always give from your overflow."

Miranda gives Council and Guidance for the Mind, Body and Spirit. With a background in Nutrition and Energy work, Miranda is the Creator of 'A Woman's Truth' and 'The Spirit of Energy', an Author, a Workshop and Retreat Leader, a Reiki Master and Yoga and Meditation teacher. Miranda studies under the guidance of her Beloved teachers Rod Stryker and Adyashanti.

To speak with or follow Miranda, please call or visit:

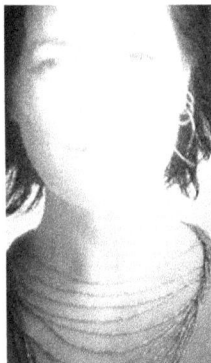

Phone: 626~798~6544
eMail: Info@MirandaJBarrett.com
Website: www.MirandaJBarrett.com
Facebook: Miranda J Barrett
Twitter: MirandaJBarrett

ABOUT HELENA
A visionary artist.

Helena Nelson-Reed is a visionary artist whose primary medium is watercolor. Born in Seattle, Washington, she was raised in Marin County and Napa Valley, California and today lives in Illinois. A largely self-taught artist whose educational emphasis and degree is in psychology, Nelson-Reed's primary focus is exploring the collective consciousness and the portrayal of archetypal imagery in the tradition of Carl Jung and Joseph Campbell. Rendered in luminous watercolor technique often described as ephemeral, Nelson-Reed's paintings are created in extraordinary detail, pushing the medium of watercolor past the usual limits. Her work may be found in private collections, book covers, magazines and CD covers. Nelson-Reed also has a line of jewelry, calendars and greeting cards.

Helena's Mission:

My images can be interpreted many ways, and for some will serve as portal to the mythic landscape. Descriptions providing background about each painting are available by request. Navigating and translating myth into contemporary wisdom is the traditional way of transmitting information though a shamanic and multi-cultural practice.

Myth, fairy, folk and spiritual lore describe divine beings and supernatural life forms arriving unbidden and disguised. In our earthly dimension, mortals often play similar roles in the lives of one another. Destinies and energies collide and interact, visible and invisible forces are at work. The mythic realms are timeless, offering insight and inspiration. While my paintings have a positive energy, many have roots in the shadows of life experience and human psyche; like the lotus blossom rooted in pond mud. For many, life is one challenge followed by the next, like beads on an endless string.

Take heart! Like goddess Inanna, one may navigate the underworld, move through dark places yet return to the realms of light battle scarred but wiser, richer for the experience. Read the ancient tales, the great mythic literature; draw strength, for they are repositories of wisdom.

Visit Helena's website for her art, purchase information and art to wear jewelry:

eMail: HNelsonReed@Gmail.com
Websites: www.HelenaNelsonReed.com
www.etsy.com/shop/HelenaNelsonReed
Blog: www.dancingdovestudio.blogspot.com
Facebook: MorningDove Design By Helena

MIRANDA'S WORLD
*Ways to stay connected
and aligned with your truth.*

BOOKS:

A Woman's Truth
A life truly worth living.

Priceless teachings reveal your transformational
journey ahead. Obstacles to self-care are explored
as clear and loving intentions are conceived.

The Grandeur Of Sleep
Permission to rest.

Miraculous benefits are realized as the worlds of sleep,
relaxation and rejuvenation are explored and deeply honored.

Nourishing Nutrition
Reclaim your health and vitality.

Reap the bountiful rewards while eating as nature intended.
Claim your health and vitality with these simple,
yet powerful tools to nourish and heal your body.

Embodying Movement
Ground your whole being.

Restore balance in your life. Discover how to embrace
your whole being through the life-enhancing benefits of body movement.

Body Care
Cherish your body as a temple.

Learn to honor your extraordinary body
as a living temple and listen to the healing messages she whispers.

Feminine Power
Fully access your supreme birthright.

Welcome and reclaim this intrinsic privilege while living
in harmonious balance between the masculine and the feminine.

The Abundance Of Wealth
Receive the gifts of prosperity.

Understand the energy flow of prosperity and weave
the threads of abundance throughout the tapestry of your life.

Find Your Authentic Voice
The courage to express who you truly are.

Your greatest ally is born
when you courageously speak your truth and claim your unique power.

Loving Yourself
A love affair with the self.

As you become highly attuned to your own needs,
allow love to lead the way. Grant yourself permission
to honor and express your heart's truest desires.
Love yourself, no matter what.

Living A Spiritual Life
Ground your divine essence here on earth.

Discover what spirituality means to you, by consciously
living between the two worlds of the sacred and the mundane.

Service As A Way of Life
Ignite the fire of love to truly be of service.

By utilizing the gems of exquisite self-care
on a daily basis and honoring your truth, your mission of service is born.

The Crowning Glory
Fully Rejoice in Being You.

A celebration overflowing with love,
blessings, grace and gratitude. Stand confident within
your truth as your mind begins to serve your heart.

The Food Of Life
The versatile vegetable.

More than just a cookbook,
a comprehensive guide for nourishing your life.

Reiki
The spirit of Energy.

An insightful guidebook full of wisdom
which introduces you to the potent and healing world of Reiki.

CARDS:

Inspiration Cards
A daily Spiritual Practice.

Sixty-Five cards with simple yet inspirational qualities
to live by and an insightful guidebook to lead the way.

CD'S:

The Grandeur of sleep and Rejuvenating Rest

An ancient healing art of rest and relaxation.

Simple yet profound practices, which alleviate stress and tension allowing your mind, body and spirit to heal, restore and replenish.

TO ORDER PLEASE VISIT:

www.MirandaJBarrett.com
www.Amazon.com

*All books are available in printed or eBook form.

TESTIMONIES

to 'A Woman's Truth' teachings.

"If you have the opportunity to experience Miranda, take it. Being immersed in her books is a magical experience. She's part guide, intuit, healer, teacher all rolled into one extraordinary package! The beauty of Miranda is that you have a deep knowing that she lives the principles that she teaches in 'A Woman's Truth'. These books bring you a feeling of safety and your life will be changed and transformed."

Ingrid ~ Rise Up Queens Founder and Coach ~ Ojai, CA

"It is the strangest phenomenon. It seems as though for years, I have needed to give myself permission to truly love myself and prioritize my own self-care. In Miranda's 'A Woman's Truth' books, no stone was left unturned. Every area of my life and every aspect of my being was transformed."

Carol ~ Art Therapist ~ La Cañada, CA

"The experiences of 'A Woman's Truth' books are just one gem after another. Thank goodness there is space given and permission granted to fully embody the richness of all the teachings."

Lucy ~ Translator ~ Santa Monica, CA

"A Woman's Truth' is an insightful series of books that helps to support women through issues that are specific to us. Let us face it, women really need support, especially now. Miranda is a knowledgeable person. When she shares her perspective, you certainly feel supported."

Katie ~ Teacher ~ Altadena, CA

www.ingramcontent.com/pod-product-compliance
Lightning Source LLC
Chambersburg PA
CBHW080524110426
42742CB00017B/3223